IN

ANNE HINE

CinnamonPress
INDEPENDENT INNOVATIVE INTERNATIONAL

Published by Cinnamon Press
Meirion House,
Tanygrisiau
Blaenau Ffestiniog,
Gwynedd, LL41 3SU
www.cinnamonpress.com

ISBN: 978-1-910836-69-9
British Library Cataloguing in Publication Data. A CIP record for this book can be obtained from the British Library.

Designed and typeset in Palatino by Cinnamon Press.
Cover design by Jan Fortune.
Printed in Poland
Cinnamon Press is represented in the UK by Inpress Ltd and in Wales by the Welsh Books Council

Acknowledgements

These poems have appeared in the following publications:
Low Force, *Rewriting the Map*, Vane and Shore Women Press; Day at Miyajima , July, Night Garden ,I'll Sing my Gratitude, Diamond Lil, Mother Decrees, Lines of Communication, Observations on a picture by Burn-Jones, Passing Through, Parlour Conversation, Loaned, Cry of the Ravaged, Word Perfect, Leaving, Counting. *Trio and other Poets,* Cinnamon Press; Memory Net, *The Eye of Temenos*, Ek Zuban; The Dove Marine Laboratory, runner up in James Kirkup Poetry Competition. Red Squirrel Press; Charlotte's Lament, Cinnamon Press; In Praise of Woods, *Northbound,* Vane Women Press.

Contents

A.M.D G.

These poems are dedicated to all who love life
and wish to capture those incidental moments,
with my thanks to the many who have helped to shape them.

Incidentals

Phoenix

You appear in the darkest hour,
the bleakest moment, when all is lost.

Unlooked for, you are there, rising out of ashes,
your plumage ruby-red and gold, shades of magenta,
purple, edged with gamboge.

Like entrancing ideas, you hover, so I many absorb
your meaning, then disappear in light.
I chase you with questions, as I do every teasing thought.

I would hold you back, call you by name,
Ziz in Hebrew, Kokko in Finnish, Anglia Huma,
Sumurgh in Persian, but you, firebird will not stay.

What message do you bring, Fenhuang, mistress to the dragon?
From the centre of the flame will you suffuse
us with new energy, bring a Second Coming?

How is it that you, born out of the heart of heat
do not have a single singed feather?

Low Force

Unbearable beauty of shine
after rain's rinsed the country;
leaves, bright, brittle and bronzed
hang gold medals against
fir green and grey rock.

An air-fresh smell of leaf-rot
and water damp-earth;
silence lost in river's
rush over rocks, busying
round bends, bubbles dance
like baubles on the surface
to take some naiad's fancy.

And we three gaze
and gaze, *allow the now*
into our slow beings,
become imbued with beauty.
Tread carefully down the slope
bearing such treasure.
Cross the blue, one-man bridge,
whilst impatient lads whoop
waiting their turn, taking
energy from the swift water.

Night Garden

Borrowed light from the road emphasises shadowland
as though trees had added kohl to outline beauty,
greened up leaves for the occasion,
making the garden inviting. Air-frost sugars the pergola,
leaves and fruit hang, full of promise.

Humans sleep, the night inhabitants, clothed
in darkness, make themselves invisible.
It is stiller than a still life; the arch
through the hedge looks for an entrance, but moon's
spotlight is not switched on, the players unrehearsed.

In the morning the gardener's whistle wakes me
as he calls the birds to breakfast.
Night's vision is swept away
dead leaves on the lawn and fallen fruit.

Porto Heli

I love the edginess of this place where sea meets fingerlings of land
the hiss kiss of turning waves on summer days
or thunderous roar when wind hurls waves against the shore.

The long sweet scented white-glare walk to town
for picnic things, the great green mounds of water-melons
and other fruits that tempt the eye.

Home again I read and look, read and look,
take in the sapphire sky and turquoise sea,
the gaudy Bourganvillia reclining on the walls
seducing bees and eyes alike.

Watch ants get drunk on melon juice
turn in ever smaller circles, come back for more,
until larger brothers turn out and bear them home.

I have in mind a treatise on the common gecko
how he sucks himself up walls on tiny pads,
hanging from the highest point sees the world
through swivel eyes as though the view
is somehow safer upside down.

Sun on the Sea

Sun on the sea scalds the eyes.
The silvery white sheen sparkles
enigmatic in its meaning.
The water, warmed, is unaware
of the shining on its wavelets
in the constant wearying movement.

Caught in a caress, a cause of content,
silver-backed fishes, weave this way and that
in the sudden floodlight of their secret space.
All is glitter, shimmer and glorious
without meaning, yet heart-filled awe
overcomes me, in the endlessness of the path
to an unknown place—the urgent onwardness of it all.

Tuscan Backcloth

Terracotta tumbled hills dotted
with green pencil and umbrella pines
announcing boundaries and new ways in.

Wheat fields climb to golden heights;
vines flourish on the rougher ground
and there's the summer glut of zucchini,
melons, oranges, lemons, peaches and nectarines.
In the distance silvered olives grove together
ancient twisted trees still yielding plenty.

Old ladies in black shuffle down the street
for bread and meat, knowing how to feed
their man is all that counts. Youth
and beauty flaunt themselves on Scooters
zoom about like scatty flies
before city's call, and they move on.

A Day at Miyajima

Life teems along the main street
while the sea laps against the Temple gate.
Deer steal the neatly packaged cookies
from the backpacks of unwary tourists
and the sun beats down. We choose a restaurant,
eat the local delicacy, to the sound of a different tongue.

Observe the empty Noh theatre, imagine
the stylised plays where actions are words.
Wander through the redness of the Shinto Shrine
watch the sunlight bob on restless waves.
Take our fortunes from the wheel
hang the unlucky on the tree of intercession.

We rest inside the Japanese Long House
where summer sun makes menacing patterns,
inky and black, on the ancient and bleached floor.
Dust motes, like past presences, fill the empty space
though the elders are heard no more, the Shogun gone.

July

Podding beans from their soft wool beds
slothful as teenage lads
loathe to leave their pits.

The sharp pop of pod
the searching thumb
as bean after bean

drop in the bowl
await their fate
in fast boiling water.

Grit in the finger nails
and a fecund smell of green.
Summer is here.

The Birthday Party

After reading Wislawa Sczymborska

- How lovely to see you, how long has it been?
- You're never seventy, unbelievable
- He looks good for his age—had an easy life
- She told me he'd left her, was living on his own
- There's a pattern to that
- Is the food ready I'm starving
- My goodness the table's groaning
- Jolly good spread I'd say
- What can I get you, don't worry I'll fetch it
- Are they ready for dessert yet?
- So this is where you have been hiding
- What happened to Jack, oh he left did he
- Always thought that would happen
- Have you been away?
- I thought you lived in Ireland
- Doesn't she look incredible?
- Isn't the garden lovely, mine's a mess
- What did you say to that?
- You can only go upstairs if Poppa's with you
- She was as much use as a chocolate fireguard.
- People are leaving and we haven't cut the cake
- Raise your glass to the birthday boy
- It's great, you must come and see us soon.
- Look at that table
- God what a mess.

Cafés are for Cynics

The station café was fugged up with smoke
it was difficult to see where you were;
then I found you at the table in the corner,
near that dubious old bloke slurping
tea from a saucer with great relish.
Within the hubbub your grim earnestness
struck a chord in me and I must confess
I felt I must raise the tone, embellish

my life with blessings I could describe
in a brittle voice that might deceive you
into thinking all was well; and that we too
had made the right choice, though my sad heart cried
out for the life we had shared in the past.
Happiness that breeds nostalgia does not last.

Happiness

I am filleted, translucent, no colour,
no people, alone in light, no shade
no ambience, no silhouette, no time
no moment, only now, no transformation,
only more of what was before,
yet no before, no after, without beginning,
no end, on and on, only now.
I am filleted, translucent and delicious in my being.

I'll Sing my Gratitude

Thank you for wanting to help.

Thank you for coming in to see what you could do
for off-loading your present state of woe.

Thank you for accepting that free counselling session
with such good grace.

Thank you for not being there when you were needed.

Thank you for cutting the bread
the only thing you did.

Thank you for doing it out of sight
being unaware of what I might have done with that knife.

Thank you for having another engagement
that meant you had to leave early the next day.

Thank you for forgetting to leave your address.

Time Healing

She died the day before yesterday
the woman who caused me so much grief.
How time irons out the creases of the past.

Even now my anger erupts
although it's over, done with.
How grudges are like sinking sands.

I did not wish her ill, but at the time
annihilation would have been too good for her.
How wishes are long lost sighs.

I tried to make it up in a Roman taxi
but her mind was full of other things.
How remorse is an unsafe anchorage.

We came to an accommodation
could smile and greet each other coldly.
How trying to please is like a fawning dog.

What to do with all these wretched feelings?
Abandon them like garbage to oblivion.
How taking leave is like being pruned.

Do I forgive her?
I'd like to think I could.
How forgiveness is a new beginning.

And as we bury her
can I bury all that happened in the past?
How I hope that both of us will rest in peace.

Paris Metro

She would go it alone, pack on back, striding out
down the Metro steps in Paris;
had me puffing behind her, worried,
her eyesight wasn't good.
Next stop London then Manilla.

I shouted her name, willed her to stop.

Wound up, she stepped over the edge,
fell on the track, lay, a crumpled heap
for an eternity—I looked, an eye opened
DO NOT MOVE hairsbreadth to the live rail.

Four young men stood on the line
daring trains to come in…..
wait until the electric's off.
Pompier at hand she is taken up.

Gendarmerie question me
stretch my knowledge of French.
Was it on purpose?
Non, *non, merci,* hot tea?
Non, its just she doesn't see so well—she's 83
Are these her belongings?
Why does she have two passports?
Where was she going?
Are you in charge?
All I want to know is where she is.
Eventually I am allowed to go,
two packs on my back.

Taxi, taxi, *Hopital Ste Geneviève,* I command
Adrenalin flows.
No broken bones
abrasions cleansed.
I'm fine to go she says

Diamond Lil

Red-faced, raw-boned, loud mouthed
Lilian was to be feared and loved.
She washed and cleaned for them
cooked for them, minded the children.

Her yellow teeth fell out regularly
finally at twenty-two, dentures
clacked in disapproval as she chewed.
Her thin and mousey hair tied
in a headscarf, wartime style,
apron made of squares of former garments.

She slapped around the house in old
cloth slippers, fag hanging
from the corner of her mouth.
Her large hands, made beds,
smacked legs, soothed the children's
cuts and bruises, were rarely still.

She was careful of the Doctor
'cos' he's been a POW in Japan
'ad a bad time she'd whisper.
Easy with her Missis—her employer
who would say, when Lilian was not about,
Our Lil's a diamond I wouldn't be without her.

Mother Decrees

that in this house there will be no spices,
no cinnamon, no vanilla, no cloves
and especially no ginger.

Here we eat plain food, add a little salt,
eat nothing that raises body temperature.
For we have learnt

that a sweet tooth leads to perdition,
that biscuits break more than your teeth,
that gingerbread men cause more than indigestion

that gingerbread houses will consume you
just as it did with her children.

Memory Net

Anash's net is flung to the sky

trawls the blue depth of memory
hangs over this empty land that once heaved with industry.

Its steel mesh catches the sun, remembers, how
as a white hot stream, it burst from the Bessemer's belly.

Raindrops hang, like sweat on the welder's face,
fall to the sterile ground.

The East wind plays this Aeolian harp
plucking music composed by the spheres,

soothing the pain of terrible loss,
allowing for new expectations.

The unfurling net forms a trumpet of hope
whose silent notes summon the future.

We stand on the cusp of what is to come
on Temenos, anointed by toil.

Two Sides to Temenos

I don't want to know how much steel was used in its construction
        I want to wonder at its creation.
I don't want to know how much it weighs.
        I want to wonder at its apparent lightness.
I don't want to know its tensile strength pound to square inch
        I want to wonder at its elasticity.
I don't want to know how each angle was minutely computed
        I want to wonder at its flowing coherence.
I don't want to know how many posts support the structure.
        I want to wonder at its power to embrace.
I don't want to know the price of this art
        but pay homage to Kapoor's imagination..

Lines of Communication

Nowadays I can intrude on another's life
with an immediacy that frightens me,
almost no pause for thought,
fine in an emergency, but day to day an imposition
that like a baby's cry, demands an answer now.

No intermediary to say the line is down.
No friendly burr-burr of line being sought.
No ugly sound marking line engaged.
No protection of just not answering the insistent ring.
No privacy in which to hear our conversation.

Fingers tap out words before mind is put in gear.
Do I need to know the cat's been sick again
or little Georgie's not yet potty trained,
or your book on architecture is so great?
This instant age needs to learn to wait.

Words on a tablet want for tone
I long to hear your voice however amplified.
On screen your words appear sanitised
exempt of touch and taste and smell of you.
Their very silence mocks communication.

Dove Marine Laboratory at Cullercoates

You are stardust more ancient than the sun.

The room is dank, reeks of seawater, drips worse than Chinese Torture.
I think of Satie's notes, cheer-up, this is half a Victorian viewing room
I should be looking from above at these tanks of shoreline creatures.

Your brain a cream rose of Nudibranch ova.

Spread-eagled over rocks, common starfish are striking attitudes
or fighting for their territory. Fully present in each leg, they regenerate.
My nerves are set on edge to think of them.

Your heart a hermit crab in borrowed carapace.

Here an anemone in distress hangs out a web of warning.
in another corner one is dead, calcifying, its spikes lie about in shreds.
Beware bare feet these treacherous nettles of the sea.

Your lungs dahlia anemones – white ones.

A whelk is trying to escape, whilst others are suck-stuck
to the glass of the aquarium, showing off their softer side.

Your liver a sea sloth – brightly coloured.

Sea-cucumbers are unappetising
not an ingredient for salad.
Translucent shrimps are walking too and fro.

Your kidneys two large mussel shells.

Foreign crayfish are the knotweed of this underwater garden
The indigenous species, opaque and slightly pink, co-ordinate their legs
move in a stately fashion like giraffes.

Your ears are cockle spirals.

Blenny fish are preening in dark places, their vanity knows no bounds,
smaller creatures live off their never ending combings.

Your pancreas a sieve of special sponge.

Lobsters stand guard along the tank-edge, hide magenta feelers.
The eastern colours of their plated armour provides disguise
as they blindly graze along the rocks, avoiding all marauders.

Your eyes evolved from luscious plankton.

I wish I had their vice-like claws to hold all this information,
their muscular tail to move me on a little faster.

You, who thought yourself a single entity
now find yourself a crowded colony.

Just to think , how we all came up, and out of water.

'There is no Cyclone' Michael Fish

It howled round the walls all night
like some monster seeking revenge
smashing into everything in its path.
Impossible to sleep with this war outside.

It must have come to an end—
I remember waking in the morning
to a pale blue sky and a wobbly feeling
like after an anaesthetic.

I made it to the window.
Here was an unknown world—
the garden full of pulled up plants
pots strewn, runner beans running groundwards.

The top of the Cypress hanging broken.
Tiles lying round the house
as though some giant had left his Lego
called out to another job.

Gone the crown of trees that landmarked home
some gigantic tantrum had tossed them like matchsticks.
Morning News reported the storm battering its way through the South
blocking roads, railways, felling pylons, outing electricity.
I heard all this as I put the kettle on and wondered
was our road closed, would school be open?
Unsure that I could face more wrath.

Alabaster Heads

After a visit to Jaume Plensa Exhibition

Please enjoy but do not touch
Alabaster is very sensitive.

Here is a room full of young beauty caught in stone
a repose that quells anxiety.

My fingers itch to touch
to trace the line from forehead to cheekbone.

Their eyes are closed, their inner space well-guarded
intent upon an interior wisdom, to serve the world with gentleness

I would stroke their rough-hewn cheeks
enhance their youthful beauty with a patina of love.

Their closed lips, ripe with youth, safeguard their secrets
but these ice-maidens do not smile.

I drink in their sweet serenity.

Like the rise and fall of tides, the room fills with the living, who stop
and look and go, not sure what to think, hungry for the more.

I can almost hear them breathe
these undead, chiselled in rock heads.

And when the people leave
the space between the heads adds a different stillness to their pose.

Observation on a Picture by Burn-Jones

Here she is again
this Pre-Raphaelite beauty, with a spun
gold veil of hair down her back.
Is a worm eating her heart?

The crown isn't that important
though she is clutching it as if there's no tomorrow
and her face isn't telling a love-story
being all white and overstrained.

The velvet gown is not quite *des habiller*
the top buttons are undone, as indeed, is she,
and there have been lovers. Oh yes,
there have been lovers, alliances, dalliances.

The worm is burrowing deep
A choice has to be made;
the asp grows more impatient.

Only Looking

I know, now, my Clarice Cliff from my Shelley,
Medina glass from Murano,
can appreciate much sought after Jensen
silver Jewellery, though I have no occasion to wear it.

What I collect in my mind are those opaque
opalescent objects by Renee Lalique.

Glass bowls embossed with birds and beasts,
flowers and fish, sparrows on ashtray's edge
looking for a share of crumbs.

Delicious dishes rimmed with vines catching light
changing from pale yellow to gentle blue,
silver clocks in delicate glass surrounds.

When harassed, I take them out, enjoy
their tranquillity, the skill that made them.

Feel more contented knowing they are safe
cannot be broken or stolen,
and give their rightful owners happiness.

Passing Through

Fifty years ago it was steeply up
on the short turfed chalk Down
the view of the Weald, a tranquil world.

Leave the M25 at the Godstone turn-off
a little way on is Strawberry Hill, which I speed past.

I loved the silence, the mute harebells,
the sudden exclamation of openness before me.

Wagons gurn and rattle on the tarmac road:
white noise thrum in the car encases me.

The fresh air and the scenery
raised my spirits, spoke of hope.

I switch on the air-conditioner,
get rid of noxious fumes.

I wanted it to stay this way forever.

Though I am travelling fast, is this progress?

Wandering in the Louvre

Wandering, incognito, round the Louvre one snowy day
I found many portraits labelled *une femme inconnue.*

Whilst gentlemen, in courtly dress, were marked as *un homme*
or had lordly names inscribed upon their portrait frames.

The forgotten women had faces that were interesting
and though their names were unrecorded their influence

was lasting. I wondered if, when darkness fell
they shared their names and place in life, laughing

at their lack of appellation, their self-esteem being such,
they did not need their husband's name, to know their worth.

An Unnamed Lady of the Americas

My first encounter with them was at the Louvre
in nearly every room hung *une femme inconnue*
and here's another, I saw her the moment I came in,
statuesque against a horse that was trying to be real.

She has buttoned up her buck teeth
shrugged off the niceties of bourgeois life,
slit the seams of her riding habit,
wears pantaloons to ride astride,

dispensing with the need for chaperones
yet wears this hat that could be abandoned.
She has won against the elements
the tyranny of landscape,

against hostile natives and wild animals
against the paucity of diet and calamities of life.
Her stance shows her to be impatient,
she has far-distant seeing eyes,

a nose that inclines to the Aquiline.
She has the whip hand, and an energy
that keeps her moving through this
needle rim of the western world.

Gertrude Bell

I think of Gertrude Bell crossing the Gobi Desert
clothes sour with days of sweat
irritating dust and grit in every skin-fold.

Despite the fire's embers the day starts shivering,
the sun races through warm with an edge
to hot then searing, heat reflecting from every

grain of sand, rocks smile in expansion,
contract with pistol cracks in coldness.
The welcome hiss of the billy-can,

and the fear of a leaking skin,
tea carved from a brick and shortage of rations.
Her face is as tanned

and wrinkled as these nomad women,
as worn as the poor of Middlesbrough
whose lot she'd worked to alleviate.

The cameleers smile, jeer behind her back,
resent her demanding ways on this pointless journey
exploring their land, that they have known for aeons.

Charlotte's Lament

Taken from a letter to W.S.Williams 2:10:1848
on the death of her brother, Branwell.

I cannot grieve for him,
his going is a mercy, not a chastisement.
His father's pride and hope
until, in manhood, he took a wrong bent.

We have known the sickness of hope deferred,
the dismay of prayer baffled, even despair,
and now to experience the sudden obscure
close of what might have been a noble career.

I cannot weep from a sense of bereavement,
there's no prop withdrawn,
no consolation torn away,
no dear companion lost.

I would weep
for the wreck of talent,
the ruin of promise,
the untimely dreary extinction
of what might have been
a burning and shining light.

Such a yearning for the emptiness
of his whole existence
is beyond my ability to describe.

And I am denied even the healing of tears.

Parlour Conversation circa 1911

Of course the earth was covered by the flood,
sea-shells on the mountain tops prove that.

Such a comfort that Noah kept the animals safe in the Ark.
Hippos, Rhinos, Elephants and Giraffe, all living creatures
including the flea, kept safe for posterity.

**Mind that Darwin chap, already shoved his oar in
causing contention with his theory of evolution.**

When every thinking person knows God's responsible for creation.
Accurately computed, may I say, 4,000 years before Christ.

**What about the strata thing canal diggers talk of:
rocks millions of years old.**

Surely the Good Book is not wrong.

The more the learned argue the older the rocks become.

The Rock of Ages rocks us.

It'll require a seismic shift in understanding

We still have Hippos and Rhinos for now...

Lament

Have I missed the tissue of signs?
Have I been deaf to the poppy petal fall,
blind to the meaning of rainstorm and flood?

Now the rocks are unravelling
skeins of coloured thread lie loosely coiled
at the foot of the knot that held them together.

They unwind to a Martian Landscape.
Mesmerised by colour have I failed
to see what all this could mean?

Loaned

The matchbox comes from Kipper's Café
in Bergen, but doesn't smell of fish.
The scratchy strike is barely marked,
I imagine waxed cardboard strips
with pink sulphur heads, lying side by side.

I ease the drawer out, not a match in sight.
A single earring hides inside, a silver disc,
like a sweet-pea petal, hangs from a single hook.
I wonder whose it is and what happened to its partner
and why, like some hermit crab, its living in another's shell.

I like it for its size
        for its surprise
        because it was saved.
I like it for its mystery.

And now I have to give it back.

The Set Aside Tractor

Every combination of life's old colours found here,
years of experience side-tracked, left disabled
at this closed and peeling barn door.

You who once sailed the field's furrows,
knew the narrow twists and turns,
are put out to grass—too old to manage.

The engine's throb, killed one last time.
Long days of retirement lie ahead—
all that know-how founders in this corner.

Picturesque, the able-bodied say—
in their obsession photograph you for posterity
forget the life you had.

Breathless in summer, frozen in winter
watching the seasons change, the grass grow,
you are set-aside.

Grey Day at Saltholme

The sky's grey skirt swirls,
bends smokestack streams,
hides distant Cleveland Hills.

Colours intensify:-
the lake browned, sand island ochred
sedge edge sludge green.
Diamond drops dagger the water
as though a thousand fish were rising.

Black-capped gulls are Persil white.
A flotilla of Canada Geese swim by;
Greylags waddle to the water.
Terns scythe the air to feed their young.

On wilder banks
Moon Daisies, white and gold
purple Knapweed shout for sun
mix with rust-red Dock in flower.
June Roses cascade hedges
crimson-edged Honeysuckle beg to bloom.
Grasses flaunt shades of green.

A charm of Goldfinch haunt feeders
ruby heads, flash of golden wing.
Flip flap flip swoop Blue Tit arrives.
A coral breasted Chaffinch
flashes a white barred wing.
Green Finch meld with feeder.
A rufus-backed Reed Bunting
sable-capped, white collared
rests on a twig.

Ebony Moorhen forage grain.
-a restlessness of Starlings
are out and in, out and in.
All beneath swirl of sky's grey skirts.

Botanical Selection

Genus Fritillaria

Slender stemmed, I found you at the end of the Ginko stand
almost hidden by the off-white daffodils sucking up the sun.
Your cream bell, not opened yet, heralds Spring.
You, who are the most delicate of lilies,
hide the secret of your snakeskin markings
unwilling to reveal such serpentine allusions.

Is it fear the spots you so? A warning to the unwary
that despite you fragile beauty, you may, unwittingly, cause harm?
Or a premonition, that being picked, you'll lose your charm
and like that other garden story, end in woe.

In Praise of Woods

Woods mirror moods: the Coniferous kind
marshal lines of thought that bring a frown to the land

furrow the brow with a certain gloom.
In winter Deciduous trees drop incessant tears,

from strong branches that finger the sky
nurturing leaf-mould below.

Warm weather, Spring—a smile after winter's frenzies—
and oh the joy of young green leaf in the bluebell wood

with its fringe of beaded beauty
primrose, violet, wind flower, celandine.

Heaviness of a Deciduous wood before a summer storm
when a tetchy wind rattles the leaves, the first raindrops

patter down and we can all breath again.
For trees are the lungs of the world.

The glory and sadness of Autumn
full of heart-wrenching colours awaiting decay.

Repeating the cycle year after year
the longevity of trees that stand without complaint

and will be there when we are gone.

Snatch of the Beech Tree's Song

Here before you and here when you're gone.

My soft grey bole reaching upward, elegantly upwards.
The width of my reach the width of my grounding.
My cycles, ever regular, follow the seasons
my being puts forth all it has.

Splendid in winter nudity
gracious in greenness of new life
sumptuous in summer
strumpet in autumn foliage.

There is nothing equal to me nor need there be
all I am is what I am.

My movement , though confined, is sufficient.
My music is hushing, I am sung to,
and hummed to, plucked and sifted *sotto voce.*
What I have is there in abundance.

Here before you and here when you're gone.

Cry of the Ravaged

Every day, every day, more bodies
Senseless killing
as though spilling blood relieves pain
assuages the blood lust, vengeance
prevents the normal, necessary life
the humdrum, buying, preparing, eating.
lost in the blast of the martyr's bomb
blowing my child's hand from limb
lives lost
terror mirrored in her eyes
we're shocked into silence
I face Mecca
Oh God!
Call on Allah, peace be on his name
but the devil killing has escaped
is running blind.....
survival a lottery
I live today but may not see tomorrow
Their cause becomes our nightmare
Who will raise their voice, say
Enough.

Those Times

I lived in those times
    when war was a fact
    death a daily tragedy
    You made do with what you had, ate sparingly,
    and when you're young that is not enough.

I lived through that time
    when freedom was the cry
    do away with all constraints
    let each one go their way
    no one bears the consequence.

I live, now, in a time
    when our fathers' sins revisit us
    the abject flee from desperate lands
    risk all they have for golden shores
    hammer on the tunnel wall
    for life and love and all that's more.

Reality's another story.

Word Perfect

She never realised, up there in her little box
how essential her words were;
how much each one hung upon them
should their minds wander, or some light
catch their eyes, cause a memory loss.

This was a job, she thought, didn't pay well
but none the less a job. She was meticulous
followed each line as though reading it
for the first time, she knew the danger lay
when she had the words by heart and failed
to follow exactly what was in the book,

forgot to turn the page. She became used
to being cursed by careless players, who claimed
they knew it all, but someone coughed—put them off—
her whisper wasn't loud enough,
always her fault never theirs,
as their peccadilloes where accounted for
and hers—well who would prompt a prompter?

Leaving

My friends, I am leaving, you,
the North-East
Alice Row
the odd numbered flats,
the Engineer Brick,
and the cherry tree.

The removal van comes
boxes of books, shelves,
three chairs and a bed
are loaded up, the men sweat,
while the cherry tree looks on.

My friends,
I wish it were otherwise,
but go I must
witness the harvest moon
in a Southern place—
with you in my heart.